Hurt in an Accident in San Antonio?

(Revealed: How to lock in your best chance for maximum compensation)

By David Volk, Attorney at Law

ISBN: 978-0-9894779-2-5

Published by:
Speakeasy Marketing, Inc.
73-03 Bell Blvd#10
Oakland Gardens, N.Y. 11364

www.SpeakeasyMarketingInc.com

888-225-8594

DEDICATION

For David Jr. because being your "papa" is my daily motivation to trek to Court for a fight.

-David Sr.

DISCLAIMER

This publication is informational only. No legal advice is being given, and reading this material creates no attorney-client relationship. If you are facing legal issues, whether criminal or civil, seek professional legal counsel to have your questions answered.

David Volk, Attorney at Law
Founding Partner of Volk & McElroy, LLP
3003 NW Loop 410, Suite 100
San Antonio, TX 78230
(210) 377-1414

www.BexarCountyInjuryLawyers.com

CLIENT TESTIMONIALS

"My accident was something I would not wish on anybody, but if one ends up experiencing what I did then they would surely appreciate the personal attention that David Volk, Frank McElroy, and Michael Volk Jr. give to their clients. The insurance company tried to offer me $17,000.00 dollars initially to settle my case but once my lawyers fought them the case ended up settling to where I took home over $56,000.00 in my pocket for pain and suffering after my attorney's fee, medical bills, and all cost were paid. They also made sure my truck was fixed fast and did so without charging me extra to help with that. They are a great group of professionals, no attitudes, caring, genuinely interested in how I was doing."

– E. Rodriguez

....

Mr. Volk was extremely sensitive to the details of my case. He was able to handle the case in my absence and be true to my wishes for a fair settlement. I found his firm to be very conscientious and thorough. This case was tragic and convoluted with issues across state lines and a military aspect. All my questions were answered in total and all documents were fully explained before I was asked to sign. Mr. Volk was also able to handle my case and be available to me even though I was in another country/time zone. I found the attention to detail and availability reassuring that my case was being handled by someone exceedingly competent. I was recommended to Mr. Volk's office and have never had reason to regret accepting the recommendation. I was very satisfied with the handling and outcome of my case. **– Rachel R.**

TABLE OF CONTENTS

ATTORNEY INTRODUCTION

My name is David Volk. I am one of the partners at the law firm of Volk & McElroy LLP. We are a private law firm in San Antonio, Texas. We are a general practice firm with an emphasis on personal injury, criminal defense, family law, and patent and trademark law. I have been an attorney in private practice since 2006. I recently was named one of the Top 100 Trial Lawyers in the United States by the National Trial Lawyers Association for my work as a civil plaintiff's attorney. I am also a certified civil mediator.

Our firm's personal injury practice is almost strictly devoted to representing victims of auto collisions, 18-wheeler accidents, motorcycle collisions, pedestrian accidents, and more.

Before being licensed as an attorney, I worked for various civil law firms as a legal assistant and law clerk where I gained valuable experience learning the ins and outs of litigation against insurance companies. I have continued that learning process since being licensed as an attorney.

I greatly enjoy representing victims of auto collisions because I truly can help the client navigate through a difficult and trying time. Our office gives our injured clients specialized attention, and as a result we are very selective about the cases we handle. We only take cases where we truly believe that we can succeed for the clients and recover as much money as possible.

HOW DO YOU KNOW IF YOU HAVE A VIABLE PERSONAL INJURY CASE FOLLOWING AN AUTO COLLISION?

Prospective clients want to know whether they have a "good case." There is no way to know the outcome of a case when we get that first phone call. We can, however, suggest ways to preserve evidence from the crash to help set up your case for success.

The first thing that must be done is to properly document how the collision happened with an accurate crash report authored by a police officer. Before the police arrive, you should take photos or a video with your cell phone of the collision scene and vehicles as soon as you can after the collision.

Documentation: Ensure You Have a Police Report and the Other Party's Contact Information after an Accident

Many times after a crash the driver at fault will try and convince you not to call the police. He or she may even offer cash on the spot to avoid "going through their insurance." These are major warning signs. ALWAYS call the police immediately to report the collision. In San Antonio, the police will arrive within 30 minutes or less

(depending on 911 call volume and the seriousness of your accident's injuries on the scene). If the damage on the vehicles is minor, the officer will give both drivers a blue form known CR-2 Driver's Crash Report. The police will ensure the parties exchange correct insurance information. Having the other driver's name, address, phone number, insurance company name, and policy number are critical pieces of information that your attorney needs to open your claim. Without them, it may be difficult or impossible to have your car fixed and injuries paid in a timely fashion.

The police can also verify whether the other driver has valid automobile insurance. They will be given a ticket and have their car impounded if they do not have valid automobile insurance. This information is critical when first speaking to an attorney about your case.

Local police are supposed to file a CR-3 Texas Peace Officer's Crash Report if there is bodily injury, death, or the estimated value of the damage on any vehicle is $1,000.00 or more. Many police officers fail to file a CR-3 unless they see major damage on either vehicle. If the police officer does not file a CR-3 crash report, you should fill out the CR-2 Driver's crash report and mail it to the Texas Department of Transportation within 10 days. The form itself has the mailing address for the

Texas Department of Transportation. You can download it at http://www.txdot.gov/inside-txdot/forms-publications/drivers-vehicles/forms/crash-records.html.

Many police officers have specialized training in accident reconstruction. Having the police accurately document and investigate the collision to prove that the collision was not your fault will help you successfully litigate your case. Insurance companies often rely on the police report to decide whether to accept responsibility for the accident on behalf of their insured.

If You Experience Any Pain, Seek Medical Care Promptly Following an Accident

If you are hurt, stiff, shaken up, sore, or just do not feel right after an accident, go to the doctor right away. Right away means right away, not 2 weeks later. For high impact collisions or any immediate injury, request an ambulance to transport you to the nearest hospital. Most people do not feel the full effects of their injury for hours or even days after the crash.

Do not wait until the pain is unbearable. I get calls from prospective clients who have been dealing with pain for several weeks or months after an accident and still have not seen a doctor. You should never take risks with your health. Plenty of urgent care centers in the San Antonio area can see you the same day as your collision inexpensively. They are open after hours so you can go after work.

You can also visit an emergency room at a hospital even if you do not have health insurance or any money to pay for treatment. Hospitals are required by law to give you a medical exam and treatment even if you cannot pay the bill at that time.

If you wait too long to get treatment, it is very unlikely any attorney will take your case. It will be difficult to convince the insurance company or jury you truly were injured on the day of the accident with such a long treatment gap. *You should see a doctor no later than 7 days after the accident.* Any longer and the insurance company will discount or deny your claim. They will say that a long treatment gap means that you really were not hurt. The sooner you go the doctor the better, not only for your health but also for your case.

PREPONDERANCE OF THE EVIDENCE: HOW DOES A PERSONAL INJURY CASE CLIENT PREVAIL IN COURT?

The burden of proof in a civil lawsuit in Texas is proof by a preponderance of the evidence. In plain words, this means the jury deciding your case must believe the facts as presented by the person suing (the plaintiff) over the version presented by the at-fault party (the defendant). Some easy metaphors for this burden are shown by the scales of justice. If the scales tip in your favor, you have won by a preponderance of the evidence. Only those who have proven their case by a preponderance of the evidence may receive money from the other side.

If you sue and the jury holds both parties equally responsible (50/50), neither party is awarded any money.

For a Claim to Be Awarded in Court, the Other Party Has to Be 51% Responsible, or at Fault, for the Accident

The only way to recover any money is for the jury to find that the other party is at least 51% responsible.

Because Texas is a proportionally comparative fault State, if it is found you are partially responsible for your injuries, your recovery is reduced by the percentage of fault you share. This means that if the jury finds you should recover $10,000.00 for your case but you are 20% at fault for the accident (and the other side is 80% at fault), your recovery would be reduced to $8,000.00.

When we take on a case we have to believe that fault rests 100% on the other party. Juries can be unpredictable and going into a lawsuit we want to focus on arguing for the right compensation, rather than fighting over whom caused the accident. Cases where the fight is over the cause of the accident are called "liability disputes."

Liability disputes tend not to settle easily. Insurance companies love liability disputes because their lawyers will try to focus the jury's attention on who may have caused the accident and away from the Plaintiff's injuries. If they muddy the waters enough, the jury can find that the Plaintiff is at least 50% responsible for their injuries, and the Plaintiff recovers nothing.

In Rear-End Collisions and Impacts on the side (T-bone) Collisions, the Liability Is Generally Undisputed

If you are rear-ended, liability is almost always on the other driver. If you are at an intersection and the other driver runs a red light and hits you, liability is almost always on the other driver. Clear liability accidents are best for making a case because the police will document that the collision was not your fault, and file a report 100% in your favor. Please note we have a couple cases where the insurance company has tried to deny responsibility for a rear end or t-bone collision. That is why it is best to have proper representation on all auto accidents because you never know how the insurance company will respond. You can never assume they will be on your side, even when there really should be no question as to who caused the accident. The insurance company is not in business to "be fair" to you. They will try to deny you appropriate compensation if possible. Some clients try and represent themselves and learn this the hard way by losing their case.

IT IS IMPORTANT TO HAVE AN ATTORNEY REVIEW THE ACCIDENT REPORT IF YOU HAVE BEEN TICKETED AFTER AN AUTO COLLISION

Do not assume you are at fault just because a police officer gives you a ticket at the accident site. While this makes your claim more difficult initially, your case may not be doomed. Often people are ticketed for unrelated citations, such as a suspended license, and believe they cannot pursue a case because of it. That is not true in the State of Texas. We have been successful in keeping evidence of a suspended license out of Court.

Even if the police officer holds you responsible for the collision, you should still have an attorney review the accident report and collision facts to see if liability can be amended in your favor.

I have met with clients whose police report puts blame on them. But after further investigation, I have sometimes been able to convince the police officer to change his report to show the truth.

One client, a firefighter, was in a hit-and-run. He caught up to the other car and convinced him to pull over. They waited for the police for about 10 minutes. As time went on, the other driver became anxious and said, "Listen, here's my information. It was my fault but I really need to get going" and left. Later that individual called the police and reported the accident without my client being present. He told the police that my client hit *him* and ran. My client was unaware of this, so eventually there were 2 police reports out there with conflicting stories.

At a later time, we were able to prove through a private investigator, accident reconstructionist, and arbitration that the other driver fabricated the story. We obtained a fair amount of compensation for him because we fought hard and employed our resources when the odds were against him. Without an attorney's help, he likely would not have had the same result.

Always Contact the Police Following an Accident: Provide an Accurate Location of the Accident and be as Clear and Concise as You Can Be When Explaining What Transpired

Once the police arrive, try not to be frantic. It is best to be calm, clear, and concise with them. Do not over exaggerate how the collision occurred. When describing the accident, keep the facts to a minimum. If you were hit from behind, tell them "I was hit from behind."

Never Leave the Scene of the Accident before the Police Arrive

It is a mistake to give the other person your information and leave the accident scene before police arrive. When you drive away, the other person may call their insurance company and lie about the accident if they think that somehow money will be taken out of their pockets.

NEVER agree to allow the other person to leave the scene. If the other driver tells you he or she is going to leave, video them with your cell phone so you can prove they left the scene.

WHAT SHOULD YOU DO FOLLOWING AN AUTO COLLISION?

There are certain things you should avoid doing at the accident scene.

Avoid Prolonged Conversations with the Other Party

Avoid talking to the other driver or their passengers, other than to secure their name, address, phone number, and insurance information. While it may be a good human relations skill to make sure everybody involved is fine, talking at length about the accident the other driver is not a good idea. They can take your words out of context and try to use them against you later.

On occasion, insurance companies tell us our client allegedly said they were not hurt or were already injured before the wreck. A car accident is not the best time to make friends with the other driver or their passengers as you may be suing that person later.

After Calling the Police, Photograph the Scene of the Accident Including Both Vehicles

After avoiding lengthy conversation with the other driver, immediately get your camera or phone out and take pictures of the scene, the other car, the position of both vehicles after impact, the license plate, any injuries on your body such as cuts or abrasions, and anything else you can think of. Be your own detective when taking pictures of the scene. These pictures may be critical for your case later.

Are Photographs You Take Admissible as Evidence?

Photographs and/or videos can be admissible if you can authenticate the photo or video you took. Some courts in Bexar County allows such images and others do not. We usually authenticate a photo or video through your testimony and if the proper predicate is laid, the photo or video gets admitted. They are useful to show the insurance company when trying to settle a case. They also can be used as evidence in depositions or trial.

While You Don't Want to Prepare to Have an Auto Accident, It Is Beneficial to Prepare What You Should Do in the Event an Accident Occurs

No one ever plans on being in an auto accident, but if it happens, be smart and safe about it. Call the police, give them a clear and concise version of the accident facts, take plenty of pictures of the scene, go seek medical care immediately after, and call an experienced lawyer to assist you with filing your insurance claims to promptly have your car repaired and injuries paid.

Avoid Moving the Vehicles until the Police Arrive; Otherwise, They Will Need to Reconstruct the Accident Scene

It is best not to move the vehicles after a collision without police instruction. If you are on a busy freeway, it may be important to move your vehicle to the shoulder to avoid a second collision. You must decide this on a case-by-case basis. Make sure you are in a safe place waiting for police to arrive.

You Are Not A Doctor-Always Seek Medical Attention Even If You Feel You Have Sustained a Minor Injury

Whether you suffer a major injury or just feel shaken up, at the very minimum, ask emergency medical services (EMS) to check you out and visit an emergency room or urgent care center afterwards. Some injuries to the head or skull can be life threatening even if they are not felt immediately after impact.

Tips on Getting Your Vehicle Repaired Quickly and Promptly

There are 2 things needed for your car to get repaired by the other driver's insurance quickly after an accident.

First, they need to inspect the vehicle. Second, they must accept liability for the accident before they begin repairs. You should hire an attorney as soon as possible after the collision. Do not try and represent yourself. As Abraham Lincoln said, "He who represents himself has a fool for a client."

After a collision, you will receive several calls from your insurance and the other driver's insurance. Let your attorney handle the discussions. If you do take a call from the opposing driver's insurance, tell them you are represented by an attorney, give them the attorneys name and phone number and end the call. Both companies will want to inspect the vehicle. Your attorney will allow them to do it. They can inspect the car at your home or work if it is still drivable. The process takes less than 15 minutes. If your car was towed after the wreck, your attorney will make sure the inspector knows where your car is located and make sure the inspector has your permission to inspect the car. Insurance companies have delayed payment of vehicle repairs for days and sometimes weeks claiming they did not have permission to inspect the car.

The inspection of your car damage does not immediately mean they will pay for the repairs. The other driver's insurance must accept liability or responsibility for the collision before they will authorize payment of the repairs.

Your attorney will make sure that the adjuster has the accident report. Do not assume these adjusters are ready to work on your claim promptly. Often times it takes persistence by your attorney to get your claim handled correctly. The adjuster then needs a recorded statement, in most cases, before they will accept liability. Do not give a recorded statement without your attorney being present. Do not assume their driver will take the blame for the accident and promptly report their negligence to their insurance company. Your attorney will be proactive and persistent to get the insurance company to inspect and authorize repairs of your car.

Some repairs are usually faster if you make the claim on your own insurance policy. In order to do so you must have collision coverage (also known as full coverage). The process is much smoother since liability is not at issue because they are obligated to pay for the repairs, regardless of fault. The only drawback is that you will be responsible for paying the deductible (usually $500) at the time of your repairs. Usually this deductible is reimbursed to you several months later through a process known as subrogation if the opposing party's insurance company accepts liability for the collision.

Most attorneys will assist you in getting the car repair done quickly without charging a fee to do so if they are also representing you on the injury claim. There are also many other ways your attorney will attempt to maximize recovery during the car repairs for other things such as loss of use, diminished value, and other claims relating to the damage on your vehicle.

Bear in mind, the repair of your car is important but your injury claim may have significantly more monetary value and overall importance because it involves your health.

YOUR HEALTH IS THE FIRST PRIORITY AFTER AN AUTO COLLISION.

Don't Self-Diagnose: A Physician Must Assess Your Injuries

There are many types of injuries after an auto accident. Some are very obvious such as cuts, abrasions, and bruises. Others are more difficult to see and require in depth medical attention to diagnose. These include sprains, strains, muscle spasms, disc herniations in your spine, tendon tears and impingement in your shoulders or knees, and others. These injuries may not

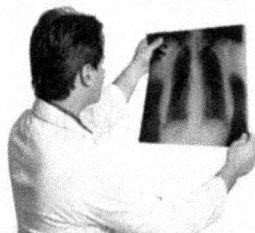

fully appear until hours, days, or even weeks after an accident but can cause lifelong disabilities.

Contact an Attorney When You Are Able to

After your initial medical assessment, contact an attorney to assist you in opening the property (repair of your car) and injury claims with the insurance company. You need an attorney's advice to know what to expect in this lengthy process. We are trained professionals who know how to prepare you for events such as the recorded statement taken by the insurance adjuster, depositions taken by insurance defense lawyers, and trials.

Calling an Attorney Early on Can Help You Avoid Costly Mistakes during the Case

We've rejected cases for many reasons. We sometimes get calls saying, "An adjuster showed up to the accident scene, gave me a check for $500, and made me sign a bodily injury release. Now, my back really hurts. Can I go back and sue them?" The answer is no. You have already settled your claim and released the insurance company and driver from any future claim or lawsuit for a sum of $500.00. Other prospective clients have had meetings with adjusters at coffee shops and made similar deals thinking they could hire an attorney later if they had regrets. Other prospective clients never went to see a doctor because they were waiting on the insurance company to say it was ok for them to go see one, much like you wait on the insurance company to tell you when the repairs of your vehicle will start.

Other prospective clients have given the insurance company damaging information when they were first injured that made it impossible for us to take their case. For instance, telling the insurance adjuster you "feel fine" during your recorded statement or initial conversation with them will be used against you when you submit medical bills. It's a natural human trait to not be a complainer and tell other people that you are fine, even when you are hurt. Other people have discussed prior accidents or injuries with the opposing party or their insurance company to the point that the insurance company refused to pay any medical bills relating to the accident.

WHEN CAN YOU EXPECT TO BE CONTACTED BY THE INSURANCE COMPANIES AFTER AN AUTO ACCIDENT?

People are usually contacted by their own insurance and the other person's insurance within one business day.

Do You Have to Provide the Insurance Adjuster with a Statement?

If an adjuster calls you, you are not obligated to give a statement on command. Advise them that you have an attorney and they will be contacted by your attorney. However, refusing to give a statement could delay car repairs. A solid recorded statement telling the truth with blame placed on the other driver can help move your claim along in your favor.

If you're not represented by counsel, tell them you would be happy to give a statement once you speak to an attorney and set up a time where everyone can be present.

You should never give your recorded statement until you have read and understood the police report. Having your recorded statement in sync with the police report is the best way to get the insurance company to accept responsibility for the accident. The recorded statement is also a great time to clear up any inconsistencies or missing information in the accident report.

It Is Best to Have Your Attorney Present for a Statement both with Your Own Insurance Company and the Other Party's Insurance Adjuster

Somewhere in your auto insurance contract, it may say you have to cooperate with your own insurance company's investigation by giving a recorded statement.

For both statements, have your lawyer present. Both statements eventually will be obtained by the other driver's insurance company. If done incorrectly, a recorded statement may hurt your case regardless if it was given to your insurance or the other driver's insurance.

All Insurance Companies Are Looking to Pay out as Little as Possible

Just because you have your own insurance company doesn't mean they are always looking out for your interests. They are still there to make sure that they payout as little money as possible.

If Your Insurance Company Believes You Were Liable, They Will Not Provide You with the Coverage for Which You Have Paid

If your insurance company puts you at fault for the accident, you will be unable to use certain types of insurance known as uninsured motorist coverage, and underinsured motorist coverage (both described in sections below).

Insurance is a business, plain and simple. No matter what they tell you, their job is to make as much money as possible through premiums and payout as little as possible by denying claims.

WHAT QUALITIES SHOULD YOU LOOK FOR WHEN CONSIDERING RETAINING AN ATTORNEY?

When looking for an attorney there are warning signs one should look for.

Not all Attorneys Have Litigation Experience

The number one thing to ask the attorney is whether he or she has actually sued opposing drivers and litigated lawsuits. Some attorneys that handle personal injury cases *have never filed a single lawsuit in their career.* They send a client to a doctor, get the medical records, send them to the insurance company, and settle the case for whatever the insurance company will offer them.

But what happens if the insurance company isn't willing to pay what the case is worth? The experienced lawyer will sue the opposing driver in order to force their insurance company to pay you reasonable money for your injuries.

Which Companies Has the Attorney Litigated against?

An experienced personal injury lawyer that handles auto accidents should be familiar with the litigation styles of most of the major automobile insurance companies.

We have sued drivers who are insured by most major insurance companies as well as a large amount of commercial trucking carriers and self-insured companies, such as Via Metropolitan Transit. The major auto insurance companies in the San Antonio area include USAA, Progressive, Allstate, State Farm, and even some of the smaller Texas insurance claims companies like State Wide Claims. Some companies are very difficult to litigate against while others are reasonable to work with.

How Familiar Is the Attorney with the Attorneys for the Insurance Companies?

The attorney that is handling an auto case should know from experience not only the litigation styles of the insurance carrier, but also the insurance company's law firm and lawyers. For instance, I know who the local law firm is for GEICO, State Farm, USAA, etc. because

I've litigated cases with them recently. Their attorneys and I have worked together, and they know I will litigate the case professionally and seek maximum recovery for my clients.

I am not saying that your lawyer should know every single person in this insurance business, but there has to be a working knowledge of the litigation field. Litigation is important because not every case can be settled with a demand letter. Sometimes you have to sue people, take cases to Court, and win.

Your attorney must be knowledgeable about insurance claims, meaning they can immediately answer questions about the repair of your vehicle and can explain to you from a medical and legal standpoint what types of injuries they have seen in similar cases. If they seem unsure about simple questions, they do not have the experience that you need for proper representation.

Not only should they be knowledgeable but they must also care about your case and your wellbeing to properly represent you. The client feels the pain every day, and their attorney should actively fight to have the client awarded not only medical expenses and lost wages, but also physical pain, mental anguish, and other damages.

While Most Personal Injury Cases Settle, You Should Still Retain an Attorney That Will Go to Trial, If Needed

The good news is that most auto cases that have legitimate claims will settle if properly evaluated, investigated and litigated by your attorney. The cases that go to trial usually have a liability dispute or other facts that weaken the Plaintiff's case.

Look for an Attorney That Is Knowledgeable about Insurance Claims and Beware of One That Tells You Exactly How Much Your Case Is Worth Before They Represent You

Caring about the client does not mean promising a large settlement at the end of a case. An attorney should never promise that you will receive a large settlement, especially when you first talk to him or her. There are so many factors that come into play when determining what a case is worth. Most are not known until the client is done with all medical care and has a prognosis from their doctor whether or not they will need future treatment.

Do You Spend More Time Talking with a Paralegal Or Is the Attorney You Retain the One That Is Working on Your Case?

Make sure that an attorney is handling your case and not a just paralegal. Some of the large volume law firms operate like that.

Paralegals may be very knowledgeable but they should not be acting as an attorney and doing all the work on your case. Make sure your initial consultation is with an attorney and not solely a paralegal or legal assistant. Be wary of law firm paralegals or legal assistants that are willing to have your first consultation at your home or in your room while you are still in the hospital. They often feel pressure from their boss to "sign up the client at all costs." In the process they might make promises that they cannot fulfill.

What Are People Primarily Seeking When They Retain an Attorney for a Personal Injury Case after an Auto Accident?

Most people are upset about their car damage and why it has not been repaired yet. The attorney has a responsibility to explain to the prospective clients that not only is the repair of their vehicle important, but also making sure that they are thoroughly evaluated for injury.

You encounter many personalities in this business, but I would say most people that call are legitimately injured. They are very confused. They have never been through anything like this, and they are overwhelmed. The insurance company calls them and sends all kinds of paperwork that literally can give a headache if you read it. For those clients, they are looking for an attorney that can take care of all the insurance headaches, make the process somewhat bearable, and get them reasonable compensation.

Why Do Some People Hesitate Retaining an Attorney after an Auto Accident?

The number one reason people are hesitant to retain an attorney is they think the attorney will charge them a fee upfront. That is not true. Attorneys take these cases on "a contingency fee" basis. This means we do not get paid unless we win or settle the case. If we lose the case or do not get it settled, the client owes us nothing. Any amount of out of pocket expenses we have put into the case is our loss if we do not win or settle your case. If the case results in compensation for the client, the attorney is paid a contingent fee, a percentage of the recovery, plus any expenses paid to investigate and litigate the claim.

People Think They Will Receive the Same Compensation with or Without an Attorney

The number two reason people might be afraid to call an attorney is they think the attorney will take all the money. They think "if I hire this attorney and get a settlement, they will take a big chunk and leave me with nothing." They assume they will get the same settlement with or without an attorney. Sadly, many injured people learn the hard way that is not true. Clients represented by an attorney are usually compensated more fairly versus injured parties that represent themselves.

Insurance companies' statistics show that more money is paid to claims with legal representation versus those without.

I had a client that came into my office in 2009, and he was very anxious about hiring an attorney. He liked me, but he was worried. He said the insurance company offered him $4,000 and was worried that with an attorney that the offer would not change and he would be stuck paying our office a percentage of the recovery. When my office took his case, it became clear almost immediately he was hiding the true extent of his neck injury because he was worried about missing work.

I advised him to follow his primary physician's advice and see an orthopedic surgeon. His team of doctors helped him immensely. I settled his case for $134,000, the per person policy limits on 2 insurance policies that applied to that accident. His medical condition has stabilized because he had enough money to get all the treatment he needed and, in addition, he received a significant amount of money for his pain and suffering.

That's not how every case is resolved, but this is a great example of the value of an attorney's advice and expertise. Since then, he has referred me several family members and friends that were injured in motor vehicle accidents.

CAN YOU EXPECT THE INSURANCE COMPANIES TO TREAT YOU DIFFERENTLY WHEN YOU HAVE NOT RETAINED AN ATTORNEY?

Insurance companies treat unrepresented people terribly. I have seen unrepresented people have their claim assigned to a team of adjusters who share the responsibility of handling hundreds of claims in a geographic area. Without a point of contact, it is difficult for an unrepresented person to facilitate the repair of their car and payment of their medical bills. They end up being passed around from voicemail to voicemail. It can be very frustrating.

I have experienced this professionally and personally. A few years ago, I was in an auto accident and the insurance company gave me the runaround. The team of adjusters was rude on the phone and would call me at strange hours to schedule things like the recorded statement and vehicle inspection. As soon as I sent a letter of representation with my attorney letterhead, I was assigned an individual adjuster that I could get in touch with and get a call back in a reasonable amount of time. Once you retain an attorney (or are one like me), you are taken more seriously.

It is a Mistake to Try to Deal with the Insurance Companies on Your Own Behalf First, Then Try to Retain an Attorney When You Are Not Happy with the Results

As stated before, speaking to an insurance company without representation can be dangerous to your case. The longer you represent yourself in a claim the more likely you may provide information they will manipulate, twist, and unfairly use against you later.

Some people try to settle with the insurance companies themselves and then seek our services when they are unsuccessful or unhappy with the offer from the insurance company. We rarely take these cases because often we have to clean up the legal mess a prospective client made due to inexperience with insurance claims.

We took one case where a client was unrepresented during most of his treatment. We had to sue on the case and spent thousands of dollars litigating before we could settle it.

The adjuster claimed our client was untruthful about his injuries because he had been speaking with our client for months and was never informed he was seeing a doctor. The client and adjuster had months of back and forth conversations about some high priced rims damaged during the accident.

When he tried to talk to the adjuster about his injury, the adjuster said, "What are you talking about? I'm not paying you for an injury. I just paid you $4,000 for these rims."

When I was retained, the adjuster was very angry and unprofessional. He initially offered $7,500.00 to settle the injury claim. After lengthy litigation, we settled the case prior to trial for $25,000.00. Had the client hired us in the beginning, it is possible we could have settled the case for a similar amount and avoided several thousand dollars in litigation expenses. That could have meant more money in our client's pocket had he come to us sooner.

How Is the Attorney Compensated in a Personal Injury Case?

As stated earlier, lawyers take these cases on a contingent fee. This means the client does not have to put any money down as a retainer. The attorney must also invest money while the case is pending for things such as copies of medical records, court costs, deposition fees, and expert testimony fees. The attorney collects their fee and gets reimbursed for their out of pocket expenses only if a settlement is reached or a judgment is returned in the client's favor. The attorney's fee is usually a percentage of the gross money recovered. Typically attorneys will charge 33 1/3% up to 45% depending on whether the case is settled before or after a lawsuit is filed.

If a case settles for $30,000.00 and the attorney charges a 33 1/3% fee, the attorney's fees would be $10,000.00. Out of the remaining 66 2/3% or $20,000.00, the attorney would be reimbursed the out of pocket expenses paid by the attorney. Let's say the expenses totaled $1,000.00. The net would now be $19,000.00. Then the outstanding medical expenses would be paid next. Let us say the client had $4,000.00 in outstanding medical bills. The net amount due to the client would be $15,000.00.

People hire lawyers for a reason. The legal process is difficult for somebody that has never experienced it. The attorney provides the client with "the keys to the courthouse." This means the client gets the benefit of the lawyer's legal skills and litigation strategy to maximize the overall gross recovery. A skilled lawyer will fight to make sure the client's net recovery in their pocket is larger than the attorney's fee, expenses, and medical expenses. This is possible in many cases if there is a legitimate injury and the client follows a skilled attorney's advice.

What If You Are Disabled and Can't Work after an Accident, How Will You Pay Your Medical Bills?

Auto insurance companies are not required to pay money in installments as a client receives treatment. If a person cannot work, the auto insurance carrier is not required to pay their lost wages as incurred either. In Texas, an insurance company will not settle a case until they have all the medical records and lost wages information. Once a case settles, it cannot be reopened or reconsidered.

This is the most difficult part of handling these cases. Most people do not carry disability insurance that will help pay their bills during their medical care. Many people never pursue injury claims even if they are hurt for this reason. They may have a family to support or other responsibilities. Unfortunately, by neglecting their injury they may make it worse and may not be able to be compensated for it later.

Some individuals carry a form of medical bill and wages reimbursement on their own automobile policy called personal injury protection or PIP. If you have this coverage, you can submit medical bills when received and receive reimbursement payable to you. You also can collect 80% of any documented lost wages you submit. Like any insurance policy, your PIP coverage will have limits that usually range from $2,500.00 to $10,000.00.

It Is Advisable to Avoid Borrowing Money from Companies That Charge Exorbitant Interest Rates While Waiting for Your Case to Resolve

There is one other thing some clients do to support themselves financially during a case, however, I do not recommend it. They borrow money from a company that advertises as "legal funding" or "case/ settlement advances." These companies usually advance no more than a few hundred or thousand dollars at a time but charge a high interest rate, sometimes 200% to 300%. Some clients used these services against my advice and each one regretted it.

Our firm works tirelessly to ensure that we recover a settlement that will help you substantially recover from that tough economic time quickly. These cases, however, take time to resolve. Litigation cases take even longer. Once a case settles, the money can also help you with any future costs for treatment and reimburse you for your aggravation, pain, suffering, and mental anguish.

WILL YOU BE REQUIRED TO BE MEDICALLY EVALUATED BY A THIRD-PARTY DOCTOR WHILE YOUR CASE IS PENDING?

In Texas, you might be required to be evaluated by a court ordered independent doctor. This can only be done by court order during the discovery (or fact finding) phase of a lawsuit.

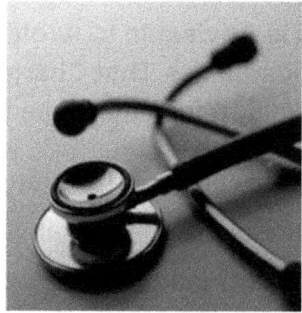

In most Texas cases I have litigated, insurance companies have a paid consulting expert, such as an orthopedic surgeon, that reviews your medical records instead of personally examining you. The doctor will usually dispute the extent or cause of the injuries during a deposition or trial. Most of the time their doctor will say your injuries are not as severe as you are claiming or are injuries that pre-existed the accident. Do not be alarmed by this. The insurance company pays them, and as a result they can be biased.

How Can an Attorney Help during a Pending Personal Injury Case?

An attorney's office can act as a form of "insurance" that allows doctors to give you medical care when you need it and patiently wait for the case to settle before the bill is paid. This is done through a written agreement authorized by the client known as a "letter of protection." Please be advised that the medical costs are ultimately the client's responsibility. This means that if the case is lost, the client will be responsible to pay the doctor's medical bills. This can make clients uncomfortable, but if they are truly injured, then they should seek the medical care regardless. It is for this reason that the attorney you hire should examine your case very carefully to make sure that there will most likely be enough money to pay off all medical bills, the attorney's fees and expenses, and the client's settlement at the end of the case.

The Attorney May Recommend a Physician That Can Help Alleviate Some Pain and Discomfort and Will Work with the Uninsured

Our office is not a doctor referral service; however, through the years we have met some of the most well known physicians, surgeons, physical therapists, and chiropractors in the San Antonio area. I always encourage clients to do their own research in choosing a doctor, but I can recommend physicians that other clients were very happy with.

We also can make recommendations on the best body shops for the repair of your vehicle and any other referrals needed to assist you in getting through this most difficult time.

THERE IS A MONETARY VALUE ASSIGNED TO MENTAL ANGUISH THAT ONE CAN EXPERIENCE AFTER AN AUTO ACCIDENT

Clients may have a difficult time coping emotionally after an accident. This is why we make claims for mental anguish, physical pain, and suffering. We highlight these damages because they have monetary value.

The tough part about the legal process is we cannot undo the pain, but we can get you paid as much as possible. That is what we strive to do every day.

Do People Have Realistic Expectations about How Much Money They Will Receive?

Clients generally have no idea what their injury is worth in a lawsuit setting. There are the few that expect large sums of money with little or no injury. Most clients, however, are satisfied at the favorable outcome they receive at the end of their case.

Every client's case is different and multiple factors have to be considered in evaluating a case.

Serious Injuries Typically Receive More Money than Do Less Serious Injuries but It Is Important to Remember That One Has to Live with the Serious Injury for Substantially Longer

I always make sure the client understands that the more injured they are, generally speaking, the more their case will be worth. If your net recovery is significant, that is good in the sense you recovered a lot, but you are more injured than is somebody who settled his or her case for less.

UNINSURED AND UNDER-INSURED MOTORIST CLAIMS

When you get into an accident with someone who has no insurance, you must immediately look to your own insurance policy to find out if you have paid a premium for uninsured motorist coverage (also known as UI). It's not mandatory to have it in Texas, so you are facing a serious situation if you do not have UI. If you do have UI, your attorney can represent you and recover compensation for your injuries from your own insurance company.

Underinsured motorist coverage (UIM) applies when the value of your case exceeds the policy limits of the other driver's insurance. In Texas, the minimum per person policy limits required by law is $30,000.00 per person with a total aggregate amount of up to $60,000.00 to cover the entire collision. Let us say you are injured and incur $50,000.00 in medical costs. If the other driver only has a $30,000.00 policy limit, you would make an additional claim under your UIM coverage to recover additional money not available by the other driver's insurance, assuming you purchased UIM. Your insurance company will step into the shoes of that other driver and the case will be negotiated and settled in a similar manner as if the other driver had more coverage.

Everyone should elect to be covered for uninsured motorists, as well as underinsured motorists.

How Long May It Take to Resolve a Personal Injury Case?

The Case Cannot Be Resolved until There Is a Certain Prognosis of Your Future Medical Costs

The time to resolve a personal injury case first depends on how long your treatment is. No progress towards settlement can be made until all your medical care is done and the doctor is able to give a clear prognosis of what your future medical costs and disability will be, if any.

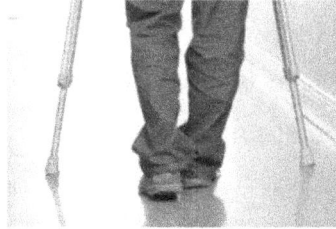

Is the Insurance Company Offering a Reasonable Settlement?

Second, it depends on how quickly the insurance company makes a reasonable money offer. Once we have submitted a demand to the insurance company, they have the option of settling right away or sometimes want to negotiate. Other times they will not make a suitable offer and try to low ball the client to see if the lawyer responds with a lawsuit.

Negotiation can go on for several weeks, to several months, to almost another year. If you can't settle with the insurance company, the next step is to sue. That process could take another year to several years.

Lawsuits start with filing the lawsuit. Next the defendant must be served with the lawsuit. This usually occurs quickly but sometimes the defendant is difficult to find or dodges service. The ones that dodge service usually know it is coming or may think they are being served with divorce papers, a warrant for their arrest, or something else. Next, the defense firm will file an answer to the lawsuit. The next several months are spent exchanging documents and information through a process known as pre-trial discovery. Either side may file Motions with the Court where issues are decided or narrowed by Court rulings. Soon to follow would be depositions or sworn testimony taken of the Plaintiff, defendant, witnesses, doctors, or anyone else that may testify. Depositions are normally done at the office of one of the attorneys. The testimony is taken under oath with a court reporter and a videographer recording the testimony. Both sides then pay for a copy of the transcript to use in trial. Depositions are usually followed up by mediation, or a meeting with a neutral host, who is an attorney, and both sides where settlement is attempted. If the case does not settle at mediation, then the case will go to trial and the jury will decide who is responsible for the accident and how much money, if any, the Plaintiff will take home.

ARE THERE OTHER DAMAGES YOU OR YOUR PROPERTY SUSTAIN IN AN ACCIDENT THAT MAY BE ELIGIBLE FOR COMPENSATION?

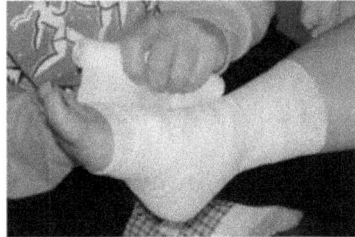

There are some types of damages that clients don't realize they could be compensated for. If you are in an accident and there is an infant car seat, toddler seat, or a booster seat, you may be fully reimbursed for a new one. I have recovered money for things such as a broken cell phone, cell phone holder, GPS navigator, work ladder, or anything in or attached to the damaged car that has value.

Diminished Value of a Vehicle

You may also be compensated for the diminished value of your vehicle. Let's say you have a 2014 Ford F150 with 3,000 miles on it and you get in an accident. You are entitled to compensation to repair the truck.

You are also entitled to the estimated diminished value or loss in value since that truck has been through that accident and a repair. If somebody purchases the truck from you at a later date, they will look at the accident history and ask for a lower price claiming it has less value. You are entitled to that monetary difference

---

between what the truck is worth after the repair and what it would have been worth had it never been in that accident. Many people do not know they can make a claim for that.

Future Lost Wages

Most people know you are entitled to past lost wages you have incurred if you missed work due to the accident. You may also receive the value of future lost wages if, at a later time, you will have to miss work for a future surgery and post-operative recovery.

Loss of Consortium and Loss of Household Services

Even if you are the only person in your household injured in the accident, your spouse has derivative claims that can be pled in your lawsuit. These claims include loss of consortium and loss of household services.

If you are injured and cannot be romantic with your spouse, he or she has a monetary claim for loss of consortium.

If you are injured and cannot take care of your children, then your children can make a claim for loss of parental consortium.

Spouses also can make a claim for loss of household services. A wife can make a claim for loss of household services if her husband cannot mow the lawn or maintain the yard, etc. due to his injuries. A husband can make a claim for loss of household services if his injured wife cannot cook, clean, do laundry, etc. These claims are usually proved with receipts from hiring professionals to do the household work your spouse normally did before his or her injury.

LET AN EXPERIENCED PERSONAL INJURY ATTORNEY EXPLAIN YOUR OPTIONS TO YOU AFTER A CAR WRECK

Most lawyers offer a free consultation on auto accident cases and will answer most questions over the phone. People never plan on being injured, but if it happens seek the advice of an experienced attorney that litigates auto accident cases. Taking the advice of family and friends may lead you down the wrong path. Do not let bad advice keep you from getting the compensation you are entitled to.

Most Commonly, after an Auto Accident People Weigh Taking the Time Off to Go to a Doctor versus Going to Work

When you face an event in your life like an injury, you need to think about the long term effects it can have. Our office is sensitive to our client's concerns including keeping and maintaining their job.

People sometimes feel guilty or strange about getting medical attention out of fear that somehow it will hurt them financially at a later time. They don't know if the medical care and time off work will cost them more money than what the case settles for. Our proven record of success shows that pursing a valid injury claim is an absolute necessity. Remember, you were injured because someone else was negligent. You are entitled by law to be paid for your injury. It is your right.

There Are Many Accidents Attributed to Drunk Drivers in the San Antonio Area

In San Antonio there is an epidemic of drunk drivers, and we have represented many drunk driving victims. The drunk drivers should not only be arrested but should be held financially responsible for their actions.

There are also 18-wheeler accidents where a company will overwork their driver or poorly maintain their trucks and as a result you get injured. Those companies must be held responsible for their actions.

Two Calls to Make after an Accident: First, Call a Doctor and Second, Call an Experienced Personal Injury Attorney

If you're injured in an automobile, motorcycle, 18-wheeler, or pedestrian accident, there are two calls you need to make. The first is 911 to request medical care and the police, and the second is to an experienced personal injury lawyer to assist you in opening your claim.

Be Forthcoming with Both the Doctor and the Attorney about the Extent of Your injuries

Do not be shy about your injury when talking with the doctor or the attorney. Be very forthcoming. Do not try to tough it out or "walk it off." You may set yourself up for a lifetime of pain and suffering if you do not take care of yourself.

We are here to help you to get through this. Call us or any experienced personal injury attorney if you, your family, or friends are injured in an automobile accident in San Antonio, Texas.

It is Worth Saying Again: Hire an Experienced Personal Injury Attorney after an Auto Accident to Maximize Your Recovery

There is a reason most people seek the advice of an attorney. Attorneys provide guidance and legal advice to help you maximize your recovery. Our firm would be honored to sit down and speak with you about your case. Our initial consultation is always free, and we do not get a fee unless we win your case. Call us today.

DISCLAIMER

This publication is informational only. No legal advice is being given, and reading this material creates no attorney-client relationship. If you are facing legal issues, whether criminal or civil, seek professional legal counsel to have your questions answered.

David Volk, Attorney at Law
Founding Partner of Volk & McElroy, LLP
3003 NW Loop 410, Suite 100
San Antonio, TX 78230
(210) 377-1414

www.BexarCountyInjuryLawyers.com

DISCLAIMER

This publication is informational only. No legal advice is being given, and reading this material creates no attorney-client relationship. If you are facing legal issues, whether criminal or civil, seek professional legal counsel to have your questions answered.

David Volk, Attorney at Law
Founding Partner of Volk & McElroy, LLP
3003 NW Loop 410, Suite 100
San Antonio, TX 78230
(210) 377-1414

www.BexarCountyInjuryLawyers.com

www.ingramcontent.com/pod-product-compliance
Lightning Source LLC
Chambersburg PA
CBHW070947210326
41520CB00021B/7097